OUR SOLAR SYSTEM

# Sun

BY DANA MEACHEN RAU

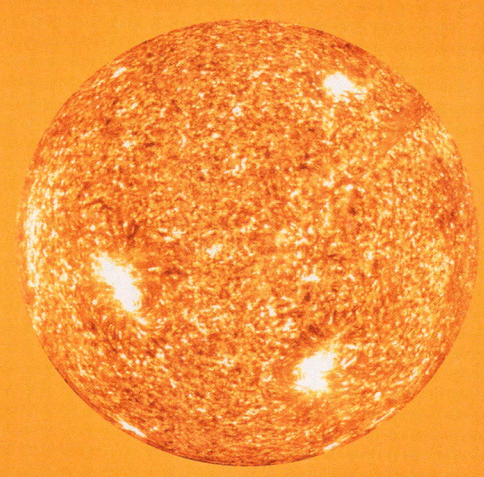

Content Adviser: Dr. Stanley P. Jones, Assistant Director, Washington, D.C., Operations, NASA Classroom of the Future
Science Adviser: Terrence E. Young Jr., M.Ed., M.L.S., Jefferson Parish (La.) Public Schools
Reading Adviser: Dr. Linda D. Labbo, Department of Reading Education, College of Education, The University of Georgia

COMPASS POINT BOOKS
MINNEAPOLIS, MINNESOTA

Compass Point Books
3109 West 50th Street, #115
Minneapolis, MN 55410

Visit Compass Point Books on the Internet at *www.compasspointbooks.com*
or e-mail your request to *custserv@compasspointbooks.com*

Photographs ©: Gerard Fritz/The Image Finders, cover, 1; DigitalVision, 3, 6, 8; PhotoDisc, 4, 5, 7, 10 (bottom), 13, 16–17 (bottom), 18, 19; Victoria & Albert Museum, London/Art Resource, N.Y., 9 (top); Bettmann/Corbis, 9 (bottom), 21; Digital Stock, 10 (top), 20; Réunion des Musées Nationaux/Art Resource, N.Y., 11 (top); Erich Lessing/Art Resource, N.Y., 11 (bottom); NOAO/AURA/NSF, 12; NASA, 14, 22, 23; Corbis, 16 (top); NSO/SEL/Roger Ressmeyer/Corbis, 17 (top); Roger Ressmeyer/Corbis, 24–25.

Editors: E. Russell Primm, Emily J. Dolbear, and Catherine Neitge
Photo Researchers: Svetlana Zhurkina and Marcie Spence
Photo Selector: Linda S. Koutris
Designer: The Design Lab
Illustrator: Graphicstock

**Library of Congress Cataloging-in-Publication Data**
Rau, Dana Meachen, 1971–
  The sun / by Dana Rau.
      p. cm. — (Our solar system)
 Summary: Describes the composition, surface features, and exploration of the sun, as well as its place in the solar system. Includes bibliographical references and index.
    ISBN 0-7565-0440-6 (hardcover)
  1. Sun—Juvenile literature. [1. Sun.]  I. Title.
    QB521.5 .R38 2003
    523.7—dc21                                              2002009940

© 2003 by Compass Point Books
All rights reserved. No part of this book may be reproduced without written permission from the publisher. The publisher takes no responsibility for the use of any of the materials or methods described in this book, nor for the products thereof.
Printed in the United States of America.

## Table of Contents

**4** Looking at the Solar System

**8** Looking up at the Sun

**13** Looking Through the Sun

**16** Looking at the Sun's Surface

**18** Looking at the Sun from Earth

**21** Looking at the Sun from Space

**24** Looking to the Future

**26** The Solar System

**28** Glossary

**28** A Sun Flyby

**29** Did You Know?

**30** Want to Know More?

**32** Index

NOTE: In this book, words that are defined in the glossary are in **bold** the first time they appear in the text.

## Looking at the Solar System

✨ Where are you sitting as you read this book? Are you in a chair? You may think you are sitting still, but you are not. You are moving at 67,000 miles (108,000 kilometers) per hour at this moment. That is because you and your chair are on the planet Earth.

The Sun is the center of the **solar system**. Nine planets, including Earth, travel around the Sun, or revolve, in paths called orbits. Some of

*You may think you are sitting still as you read a book, but you actually travel through space all the time.* ▶

*Earth is one of the nine planets that orbit the Sun.* ▶

these planets have moons. There are also pieces of ice, called **comets**, moving through space. Pieces of rock, called **asteroids** and **meteoroids**, are floating through space, too. All of these objects make up the solar system.

▲ *The Sun is a star like the ones shown glowing in the night sky.*

◀ *Comets orbiting in space are also a part of the solar system.*

The Sun is a star. Stars are made up of hot gases. There are billions of stars in our galaxy. The Sun is the closest star to Earth. The Sun is middle-sized compared to other stars, but it is the largest object in the solar system. It would take more than one hundred Earths lined up to stretch across the Sun.

# Looking up at the Sun

⋆ The Sun is nearly 5 billion years old. That is also the age of the solar system. Scientists believe that the solar system started as a huge cloud of spinning gas and dust. As the cloud spun, much of the gas moved to the center and became the Sun. The rest of the gas and dust became the planets and their moons.

The Sun has been in the sky much, much longer than there have been people on Earth. People have been gaz-

*The Sun is as old as the solar system itself.* ▶

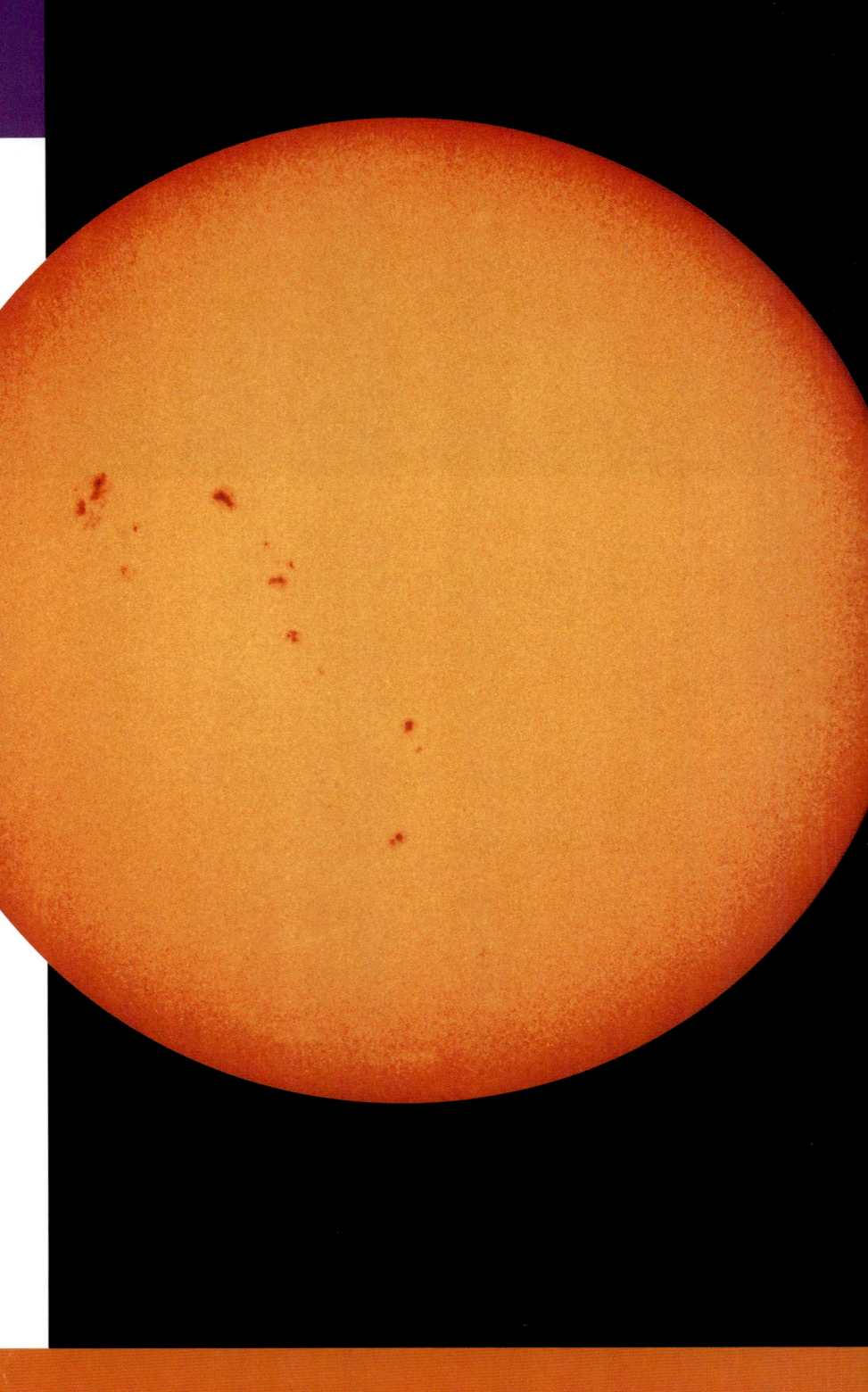

ing at the Sun for thousands of years. Many people who lived long ago thought the Sun was a god. The Greeks called their sun god Helios. The Japanese called their sun goddess Amaterasu. Some western Africans called

◀ *The Japanese sun goddess Amaterasu (above) and the Greek sun god Helios (left)*

the Sun Liza. The Egyptian Sun god was called Ra.

Long ago, many people drew pictures and made statues to honor these gods. Sometimes they lined up their buildings or structures with objects they saw in the sky. Stonehenge is a famous circle of large stones in England. The rocks are lined up with the Sun so that it shines on them in certain ways at different times of the year. The pyramids in Egypt are also thought to be linked to objects the Egyptians saw in the sky.

People believe the rocks at Stonehenge (above) and the Egyptian pyramids (right) are linked to objects in the sky.

People have always known the Sun is important. For a while, though, they did not believe it was the center of the solar system. Two thousand years ago, the Greek **astronomer** Ptolemy first had the idea that Earth was the center of the solar system. He thought the other planets and the Sun circled Earth. In the 1500s, a Polish astronomer named Nicolaus Copernicus (1473–1543) first had the idea that the Sun was the center. His idea proved to be the right one.

▲ *Ptolemy (2nd century) believed the Sun circled Earth.*

◀ *Copernicus's idea about the Sun being the center of the solar system proved correct.*

Today, many astronomers study the Sun. When they look at the Sun, they use **telescopes**, which have filters. The filters keep out the Sun's harmful rays.

It is important never to look directly at the Sun, especially not with a telescope.

*The McMath-Pierce solar facility in Arizona is actually a huge telescope that allows astronomers to study the Sun.*

# Looking Through the Sun

The Sun is so hot that nothing solid or liquid can exist there. The Sun is made mostly of a gas called hydrogen. The center of the Sun is like a large factory. There, the hydrogen burns and turns into the gas helium. It is very hot in the center of the Sun—about 28.8 million degrees Fahrenheit (16 million degrees Celsius).

The part of the Sun we see from Earth is called the photosphere. It is the "surface" of

◀ *The Sun is so hot that in its center, hydrogen burns and becomes helium.*

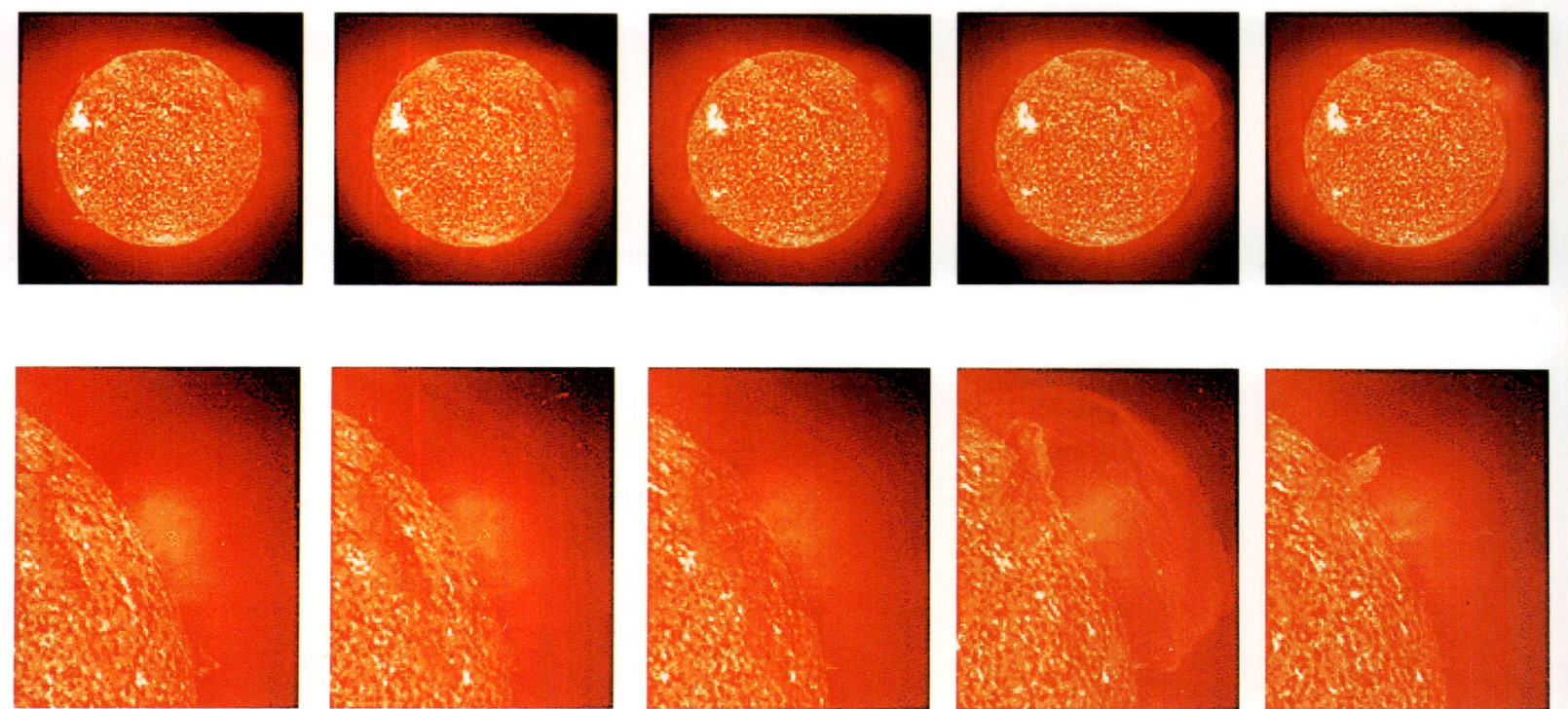

the Sun. It is the part that gives off light. The photosphere is not solid like the surface on Earth, however. The hot gases on the surface of the Sun are always moving. The surface is cooler than the inside of the Sun.

The **temperature** in the photosphere is about 12,140 degrees Fahrenheit (6,700 degrees C).

Above the photosphere is an area called the chromosphere. It is a dark red color. It spurts out hot gas. Next comes the corona. It is the Sun's atmos-

*The Sun's hot gases are constantly in motion.*

phere. Most of the planets have atmospheres, too. An atmosphere is the mixture of gases that surrounds a planet. The Sun's atmosphere is much larger than those of the planets. The Sun's corona goes all the way to the edge of the solar system in the form of a **solar wind**. The corona is very hot. It is about 3.6 million degrees Fahrenheit (2 million degrees C).

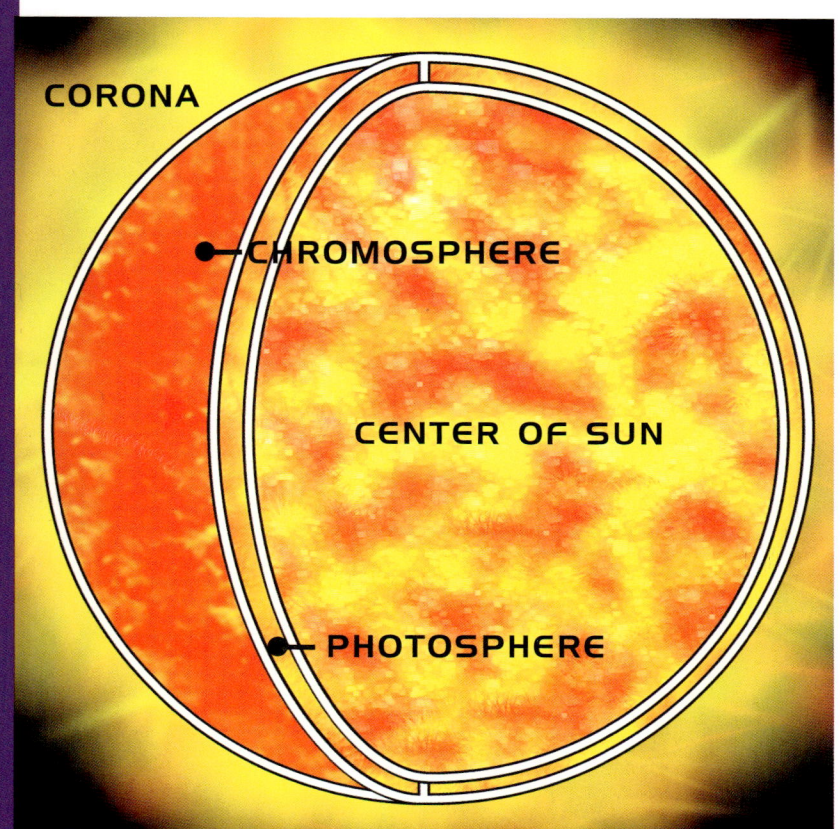

◂ *A diagram of the Sun*

## Looking at the Sun's Surface

Planets rotate, or spin, as they orbit the Sun. The Sun also rotates at the center of the solar system. It takes the Sun a little more than twenty-five Earth-days to spin once. It takes a little longer (about thirty-six days) at the top and bottom of the Sun. These areas are called its **poles**. The Sun spins this way because it is made of gas. It isn't solid, like a ball.

There are interesting markings on the Sun that astron-

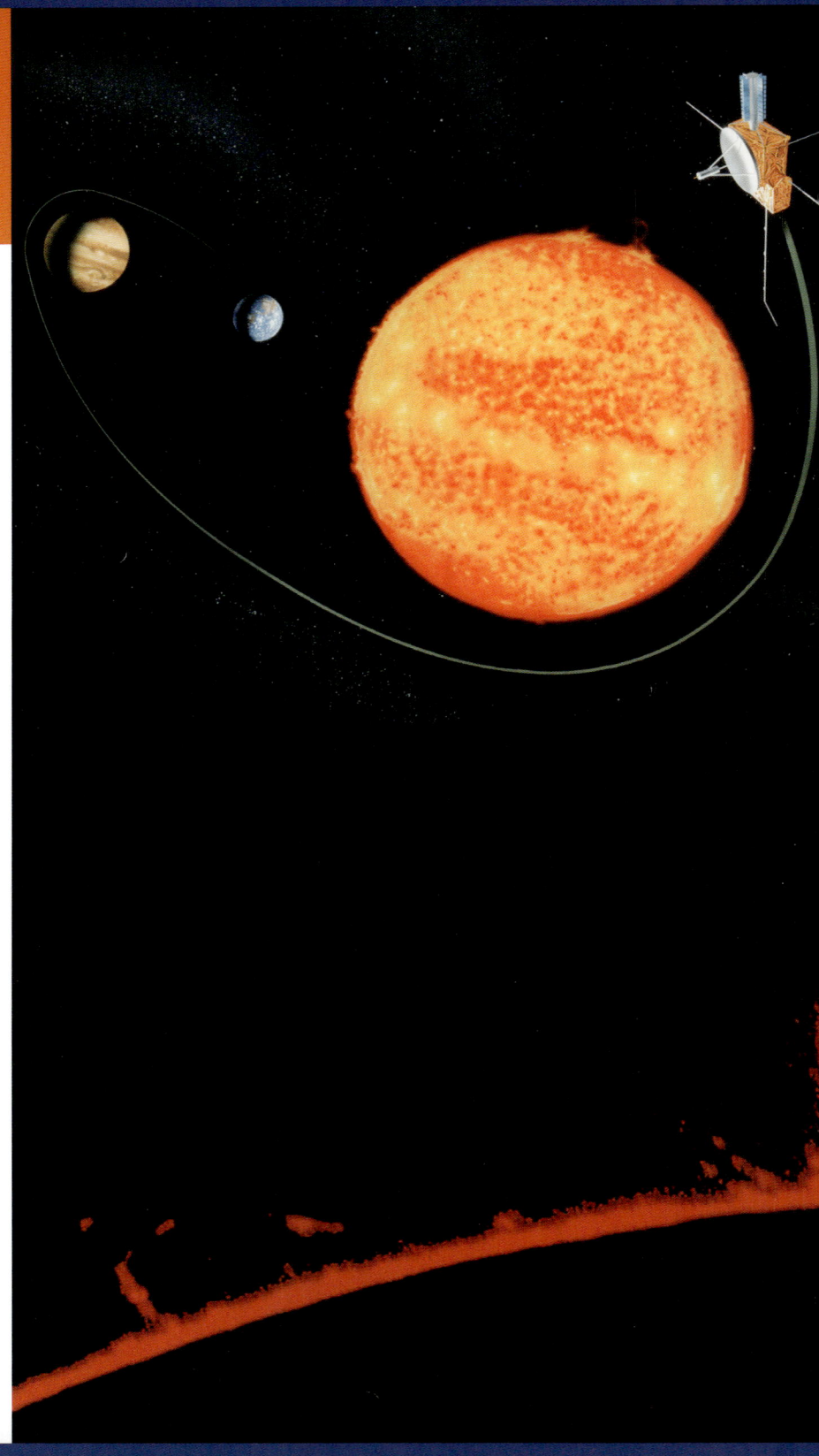

▶ *An artist's drawing of* Ulysses, *a spacecraft that is studying the Sun*

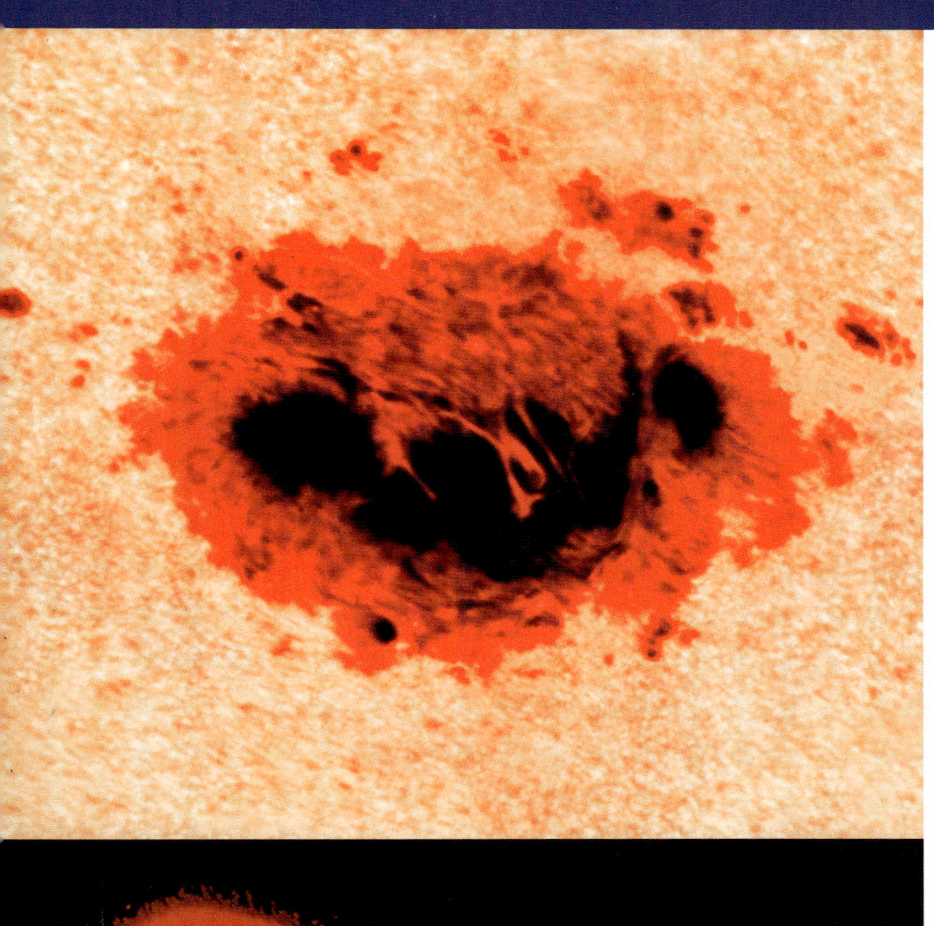

omers like to watch. The Sun sometimes has small dark areas called sunspots. They appear about every eleven years. A sunspot is a spot on the Sun that is cooler than the area around it.

At the sunspots, astronomers sometimes see solar flares. They are explosions. The Sun stores up energy, then shoots it out from the surface.

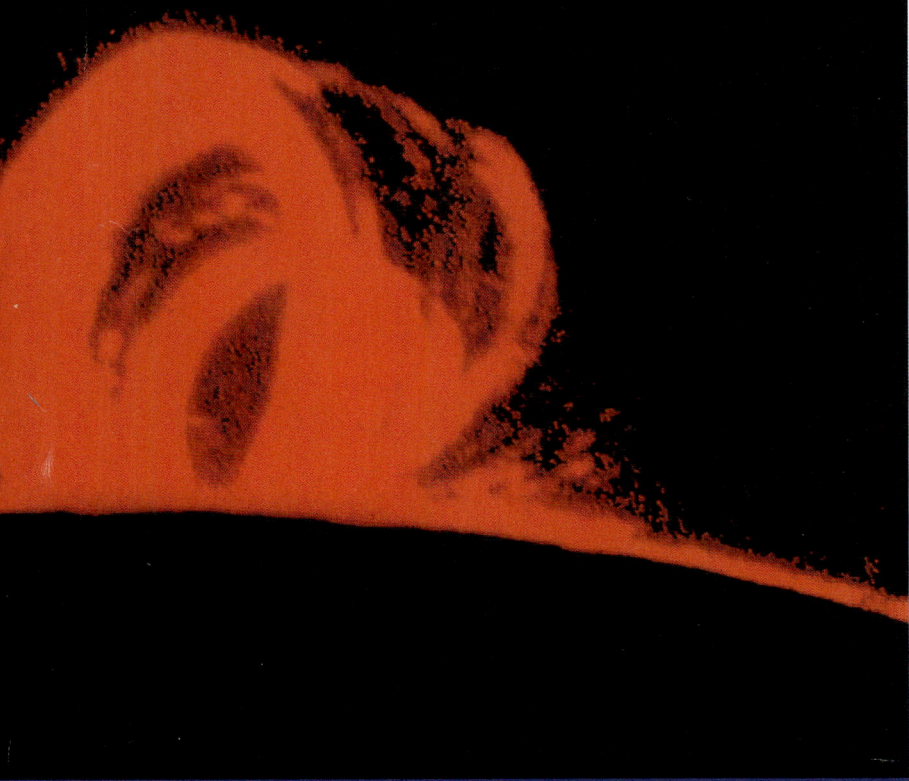

▲ Sunspots such as this one appear about every eleven years.

◀ Solar flares sometimes occur at the sunspots.

# Looking at the Sun from Earth

✦ The Sun provides Earth with light and heat. This light and heat is called energy. The energy from the Sun starts in the center of the Sun. When the Sun turns hydrogen into helium, energy is created. This energy travels from the inside of the Sun to its surface. That takes almost two hundred thousand years. Then the energy flows through the photosphere and chromosphere to the corona. The corona brings the energy to Earth.

*A solar eclipse* ▶

The only time the corona can be seen from Earth is during a solar eclipse. This is when the Moon blocks the view of the Sun from Earth. The Moon's shadow blocks the Sun's light. During a solar eclipse we see only the glow of the Sun's corona around the Moon.

The solar wind of the corona can sometimes be seen in the sky at night. Beautiful lights called the northern lights and southern lights sometimes appear in the sky. They are glowing, colored lights.

▼ *The solar wind can be seen in the form of the beautiful northern lights.*

Many people, animals, and plants live on Earth. It is the only planet in the solar system with living things. That is because Earth gets just the right amount of energy from the Sun to have life. Earth could not have life without the Sun. Green plants need the Sun to grow. Plants create the gas oxygen, which people need to breathe. The Sun causes the weather and the seasons on Earth. Its heat keeps Earth just the right temperature for life to exist.

*Without the Sun, Earth would have no green plants, and people would have no oxygen to breathe.*

# Looking at the Sun from Space

Many space missions have been sent to the Sun to study it more closely. It is much too hot for people to visit. Scientists have created special spacecraft to fly toward and orbit the Sun.

Missions to the Sun began in the 1950s. In 1959, *Mariner 2* closely studied solar wind for the first time. Today, there are many spacecraft orbiting the Sun to tell astronomers more about it. *Ulysses* was sent to explore

◂ *President John F. Kennedy with a model of* Mariner 2 *in 1963*

the Sun's poles in 1990. It is still orbiting the Sun today. It is studying the corona and solar wind, as well as many other things.

The *Genesis* spacecraft was launched in 2001. It is finding out what the Sun is made of by collecting some of its solar wind. For two years, it will collect solar wind. Then it will come back to Earth in 2004 so astronomers can study what the wind is made of.

Most recently, astronomers have sent a special instrument called HESSI on a mission to study the Sun. It was launched in February 2002. Its job is to study solar flares. Scientists are curious about the information HESSI will collect for them.

*Genesis* was launched in 2001.

HESSI's *task is to study solar flares.*

## Looking to the Future

The Sun will not last forever. Someday it will do what other stars do. It will grow larger and brighter. It will be called a red giant star. This red giant star will grow so large that it will destroy the planets closest to it—Mercury, Venus, Earth, and Mars. Then it will collapse and become very small. It will be called a white dwarf star.

This will not happen for 5 billion years. For now, people can watch the Sun from Earth. We can feel its

warmth, use its light, and enjoy its energy that gives plants and animals life on Earth.

◀ *The Sun, shown here behind Earth during a solar eclipse, will one day experience the same changes as the other stars around it.*

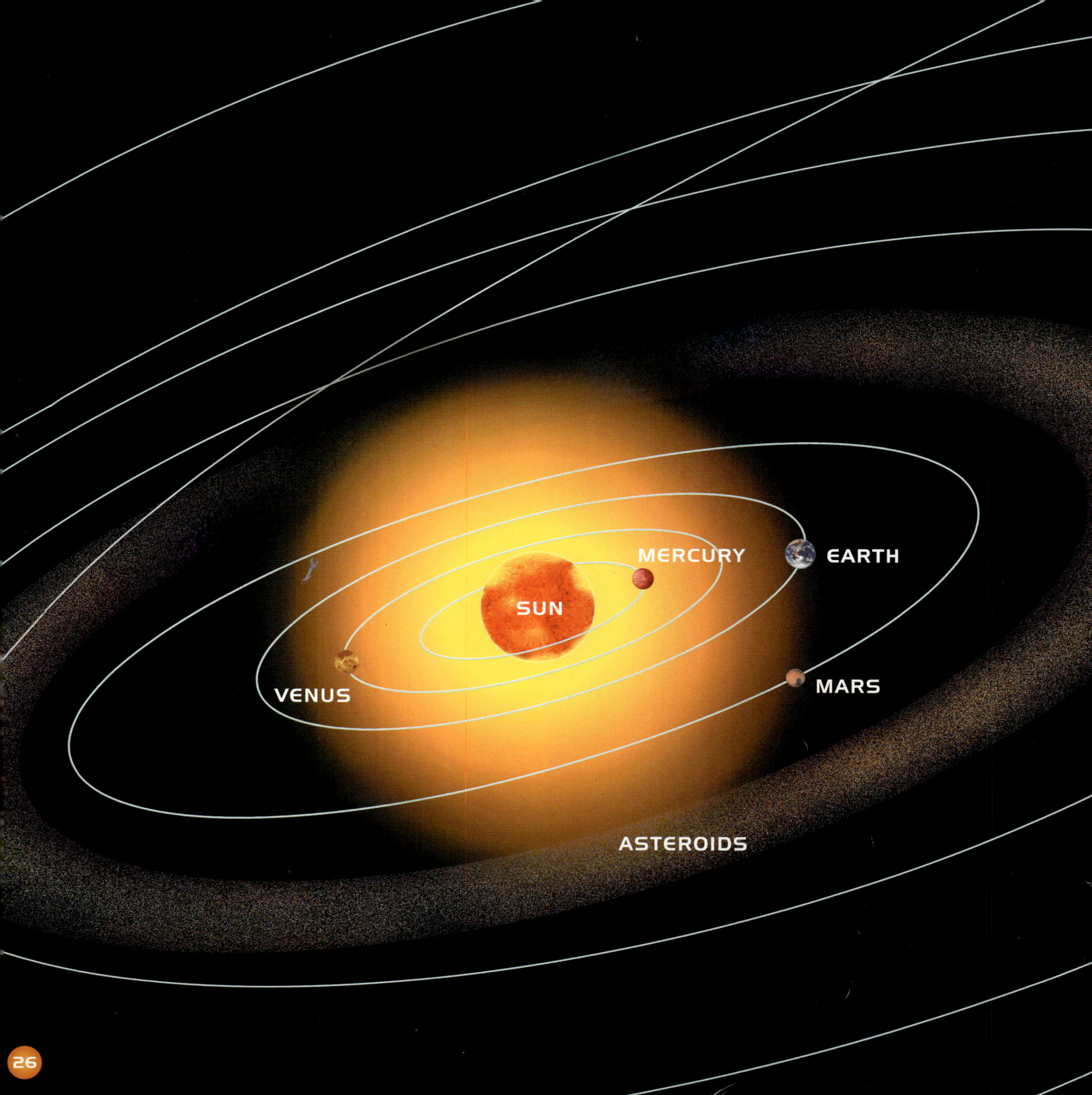

## Glossary

**asteroids**—chunks of rock that orbit the Sun especially between the orbits of Mars and Jupiter

**astronomer**—a person who studies space

**comets**—pieces of ice and rock that have long tails of dust and orbit the Sun

**meteoroids**—chunks of rock in space; when they hit a planet, they are called meteorites

**poles**—the northernmost and southernmost points on the Sun

**solar system**—a group of objects in space including the Sun, planets, moons, asteroids, comets, and meteoroids

**solar wind**—energy from the Sun traveling to Earth and other parts of the solar system

**telescopes**—tools astronomers use to make objects look closer

**temperature**—how hot or cold something is

### A Sun Flyby

Average distance from Earth: 93 million miles (149.6 million kilometers)

Number of times Earth would fit inside Sun: more than 1.3 million

Diameter: 864,000 miles (1.4 million km)

Density: (Earth=5,520 kg/m3) 1,410 kg/m3

Time it takes to rotate: 25.4 Earth-days (36 days at poles)

Structure: hot center, radiation zone, convection zone, photosphere, chromosphere, corona

# Did You Know?

- The German astronomer Heinrich Schwabe (1826–1843) was the first to discover that the sunspots on the Sun appear about every eleven years.

- The next closest star to Earth is Proxima Centauri. It is 268,000 times farther away from Earth than the Sun.

- When there are a lot of sunspots or solar flares on the Sun, radios on Earth sometimes act strangely.

- People who lived long ago were afraid when they saw a solar eclipse because they did not understand what it was.

- Many nations have sent missions to study the Sun, including the United States, Russia, and Japan.

- Earth is in the Milky Way galaxy. The Milky Way galaxy has 200 billion stars.

- In 1610, the Italian astronomer Galileo Galilei (1564–1642) was the first to use a telescope to see sunspots.

- Long ago, the Chinese believed there were ten Suns—one for each day of their ten-day week.

**Composition:** 92.1% hydrogen, 7.8% helium, 0.1% other

**Photosphere temperature:** 12,140 degrees Fahrenheit (6,700 degrees C)

**Center temperature:** 28.8 million degrees Fahrenheit (16 million degrees C)

**Surface temperature:** (Earth=1.0) : 9,932 degrees F (5,500 degrees C)

# Want to Know More?

## AT THE LIBRARY

Fowler, Allan. *The Sun's Family of Planets.* Chicago: Childrens Press, 1993.

Mitton, Jacqueline and Simon Mitton. *Scholastic Encyclopedia of Space.* New York: Scholastic Reference, 1998.

Rau, Dana Meachen. *The Solar System.* Minneapolis: Compass Point Books, 2000.

Redfern, Martin. *The Kingfisher Young People's Book of Space.* New York: Kingfisher, 1998.

## ON THE WEB

**Live from the Sun**
*http://passporttoknowledge.com/sun/sun_main.html*
For information on the Sun and how it affects Earth

**The Nine Planets: The Sun**
*http://www.seds.org/nineplanets/nineplanets/sol.html*
For a multimedia tour of the solar system, including planets and their moons

**Solar System Exploration: The Sun**
*http://sse.jpl.nasa.gov/features/planets/sun/sun.html*
For more information about the Sun and related links to other sites

**Space Kids**
*http://spacekids.hq.nasa.gov*
NASA's space science site designed just for kids

**Space.com**
*http://www.space.com*
For the latest news about everything to do with space

**Sunspots**
*http://www.exploratorium.edu/sunspots/*
For more detailed information and pictures of sunspots

**Ulysses Mission Home Page**
*http://helio.estec.esa.nl/ulysses_welcome_page.html*
For information about the *Ulysses* mission

**Windows to the Universe: Sun**
*http://www.windows.ucar.edu/tour/link=/sun/sun.html*
For more information about the Sun

## THROUGH THE MAIL

**Goddard Space Flight Center**
Code 130, Public Affairs Office
Greenbelt, MD 20771
To learn more about space exploration

**Jet Propulsion Laboratory**
4800 Oak Grove Drive
Pasadena, CA 91109
818/354-4321
To learn more about the
spacecraft missions

**Lunar and Planetary Institute**
3600 Bay Area Boulevard
Houston, TX 77058
To learn more about the solar system

**Space Science Division**
NASA Ames Research Center
Moffet Field, CA 94035
To learn more about solar
system exploration

## ON THE ROAD

**Adler Planetarium and Astronomy Museum**
1300 S. Lake Shore Drive
Chicago, IL 60605-2403
312/922-STAR
To visit the oldest planetarium
in the Western Hemisphere

***Exploring the Planets* and *Where Next, Columbus?***
National Air and Space Museum
7th and Independence Avenue, S.W.
Washington, DC 20560
202/357-2700
To learn more about the solar system and
space exploration at this museum exhibit

**Rose Center for Earth and Space/Hayden Planetarium**
Central Park West at 79th Street
New York, NY 10024-5192
212/769-5100
To visit this new planetarium and learn
more about the solar system

**UCO/Lick Observatory**
University of California
Santa Cruz, CA 95064
831/459-2513
To see the telescope that was used to
discover the first planets outside of our
solar system

## Index

age, 8
Amaterasu (Japanese sun goddess), 9
asteroids, 7
astronomers, 11, 12, 16–17, 22
chromosphere, 14, 18
comets, 7
Copernicus, Nicolaus, 11
corona, 15, 18–19, 22
Earth, 4, 7, 18, 20, 24–25
energy, 18, 25
*Genesis* spacecraft, 22
Helios (Greek sun god), 9
helium gas, 13, 18
HESSI (research instrument), 22
hydrogen gas, 13, 18
*Mariner 2* spacecraft, 21
meteoroids, 7
moons, 7, 8, 19
northern lights, 19
orbit, 4, 16, 21, 22
oxygen gas, 20
photosphere, 13–14, 18
planets, 4, 7, 8, 24
plant life, 20, 25
poles, 16, 22
Ptolemy, 11
pyramids, 10
Ra (Egyptian sun god), 10
red giant stars, 24
religion, 9–10
rotation, 16
size, 7
solar eclipse, 19
solar flares, 17, 22
solar system, 4, 7, 8, 11
solar wind, 15, 19, 22
southern lights, 19
spacecraft, 21–22
stars, 7, 24
Stonehenge, 10
sunspots, 17
telescopes, 12
temperature, 13, 14, 15, 17, 20
*Ulysses* spacecraft, 21–22
white dwarf star, 24

◂ **About the Author:** Dana Meachen Rau loves to study space. Her office walls are covered with pictures of planets, astronauts, and spacecraft. She also likes to look up at the sky with her telescope and write poems about what she sees. Ms. Rau is the author of more than seventy-five books for children, including nonfiction, biographies, storybooks, and early readers. She lives in Burlington, Connecticut, with her husband, Chris, and children, Charlie and Allison.